Franc Assisi

Keeper of Creation

1181/82–1226
Born in Assisi, Italy
Feast Day: October 4
Patronage:
Animals, nature, and Italy

Text by Barbara Yoffie
Illustrated by Katherine A. Borgatti

Liguori
ONE LIGUORI DRIVE
LIGUORI MO 63057-9999

Dedication

To my family:
my parents Jim and Peg,
my husband Bill,
our son Sam and daughter-in-law Erin,
and our precious grandchildren
Ben, Lucas, and Andrew

To all the children I have had the privilege of
teaching throughout the years.

Imprimi Potest:
Harry Grile, CSsR, Provincial
Denver Province, The Redemptorists

Published by Liguori Publications
Liguori, Missouri 63057

To order, call 800-325-9521
www.liguori.org

p ISBN: 978-0-7648-2327-5
e ISBN: 978-0-7648-6846-7

Liguori Publications, a nonprofit corporation, is an apostolate of The
Redemptorists. To learn more about The Redemptorists, visit Redemptorists.com.

Printed in the United States of America
17 16 15 14 13 / 5 4 3 2 1
First Edition

Dear Parents and Teachers:

Saints and Me! is a series of children's books about saints, with six books in each set. The first set is titled *Saints of North America*. This second set, *Saints of Christmas,* selects seven heavenly heroes who teach us to love the Infant Jesus. Some saints in this set have feast days within Advent and Christmas time, but others are celebrated within ordinary time and Easter time. We selected these saints based on their connection to the Christmas story and how they inspire us to let the mystery of Christ's birth grow within our hearts.

Saints of Christmas includes the heroic lives of seven saints from different times and places who loved Jesus. Saints Mary and Joseph witnessed the miracle of God's abundant love for humanity as our Infant Savior entered the world to bring us home to God. Saint Lucy followed Jesus in a time when Christianity was against the law. The story of Saint Nicholas was so incredible that it inspired our secular notion of Santa Claus. Saint Francis of Assisi added much flavor to our current Christmas traditions. Saint Martin de Porres is a biracial saint who teaches us about divine love for all people. And a saint of our own era, Gianna Beretta Molla, witnessed a deep belief in the gift of life.

Which saint cared for slaves from Africa? Who became a doctor and mother? What saints were present at Jesus' birth in Bethlehem? Who desired to be a knight? Which saint was a bishop of a seaport city? Do you know which saint's name means "light?" Find the answers in the *Saints of Christmas* set, part of the *Saints and Me!* series, and help your child identify with the lives of the saints.

Introduce your children or students to the *Saints and Me!* series as they:

—**READ** about the lives of the saints and are inspired by their stories.

—**PRAY** to the saints for their intercession.

—**CELEBRATE** the saints and relate to their lives.

saints of christmas

advent	**week 1**		
	week 2		
	week 3		
	week 4		
christmas	**week 5**		
	week 6		

Mary and Joseph

Lucy

Nicholas of Myra

Francis of Assisi

Martin de Porres

Gianna Beretta Molla

Francis was born in the small town of Assisi, in Italy. His father was a successful cloth merchant. He wanted his son to be just like him when he grew up. "You can help me in the store," he told Francis.

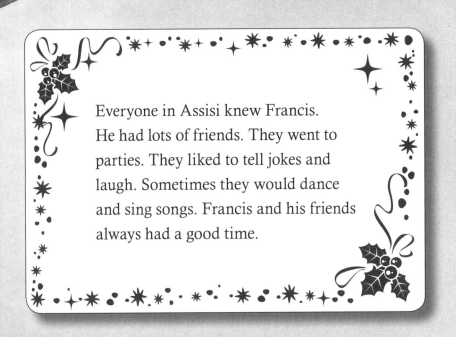

Everyone in Assisi knew Francis. He had lots of friends. They went to parties. They liked to tell jokes and laugh. Sometimes they would dance and sing songs. Francis and his friends always had a good time.

When Francis grew up he joined the army. He wanted to be a knight. This was his chance to be strong and brave. But Francis was captured and put in prison. He was there for a long time. In prison, he thought and thought. "What should I do with my life?" he asked himself.

Francis went home to his family in Assisi. He was sick for a long time. He kept thinking about what he should do. Should I work in my father's store? Should I have fun with my friends? So he thought and prayed. God would help him decide what to do.

Some of Francis' friends came to see him. "What is the matter, Francis? Let's go have some fun. Come to a party with us tonight." They waved good-bye and walked down the road. But Francis did not want to go to a party. He had found peace and joy with God instead.

A few days later, Francis met a man on the road. His hands were wrapped in bandages. Francis knew the man was a leper. Lepers lived outside the town because they were sick. The man looked very sad and lonely. Francis gave him a hug. "Here, take this," he said. He gave him all the money he had in his pocket!

As Francis walked away he suddenly felt very happy. He felt peaceful. "I should help more people," he thought. He walked to the old San Damiano Church and knelt down to pray. "God, please help me," he said.

Soon he heard a whisper. The voice said, "Fix my church." Francis looked around the church but did not see anyone. "Well, I can fix this old church," said Francis. "It needs a few stones here and there. I can do that!"

So he found some stones and started to fix the old church. He started to live a more simple life. I don't need much, he thought. I need simple clothes and food to eat. He thought about how Jesus lived long ago. Jesus didn't need much, either.

One day at Mass he heard an important
Gospel lesson. Go preach and teach.
Take nothing with you. "That's it!
I will preach the Gospel like Jesus,"
cried Francis. He gave away his shoes
and good clothes. Now he wore a brown
tunic with a rope tied around his waist.

People liked to hear Francis preach. He was kind, cheerful, and always smiled. He preached about peace and forgiveness. "Be close to God. Look at what he created for us—the sun, moon, and stars. Look at the flowers, the animals, and birds. God loves us so much!"

Soon people followed Francis. They liked his simple life. His little group soon became a religious order called the Friars Minor. They preached and helped sick and poor people.

Francis traveled to the town of Gubbio. People told him about a mean wolf that lived in the woods. "Please help us, Francis," they begged. Francis called the wolf. "Brother Wolf, you must be kind," he said. The wolf obeyed Francis and became gentle and tame.

Christmas was special for Francis. Jesus was born on this day. Francis made a manger scene with real people and real animals. There was a donkey, an ox, and some sheep. All could see the little Baby Jesus, too. Everyone celebrated with joy!

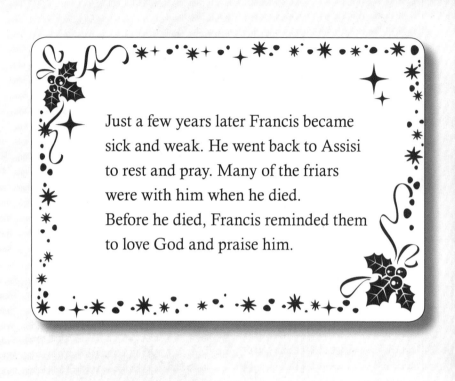

Just a few years later Francis became sick and weak. He went back to Assisi to rest and pray. Many of the friars were with him when he died.
Before he died, Francis reminded them to love God and praise him.

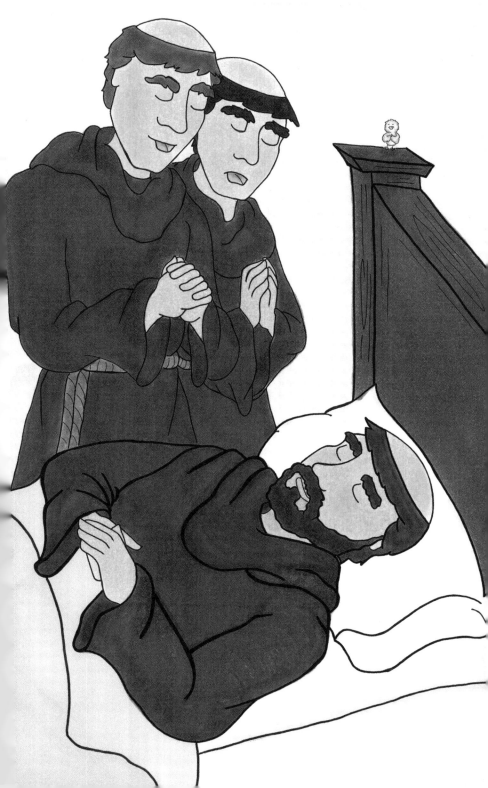

Saint Francis calls us
to look at ourselves.
Do we respect the earth
and all creation?
How can we make our world
a better place?

Francis has a message for every girl and boy.
Love God, serve God,
and be filled with peace and joy!

Dear God.

I love you.

Saint Francis

loved you, too.

He loved everything

you created.

Help me to grow

close to you

in your creation.

Fill me with peace and joy.

Amen.

NEW WORDS (Glossary)

Creation: Everything that God made—people, animals, and nature

Friar: A member of the religious order Friars Minor

Friars Minor: The order started by Saint Francis of Assisi; members now are called Franciscans

Leper: A person who has leprosy, a serious skin disease that causes sores on the skin

Merchant: A person who buys and sells items

Order: A religious community of men or women

Preach: To teach about faith, God, and the Good News

Tunic: A loose-fitting piece of clothing that is tied at the waist with a cord

Liguori Publications
saints and me! series
SAINTS OF CHRISTMAS

Collect the entire set!

LUCY
A Light for Jesus

Francis of Assisi
Keeper of Creation

martin de porres
A Beggar for Justice

nicholas of myra
Giver of Many Gifts

Gianna Beretta molla
Wife, Mother, and Doctor

mary and Joseph
Models of Faith and Love

SAINTS OF NORTH AMERICA
activity book
Reproducible activities
for all 6 saints in the series